PIRATES

Nikalas Catlow

Tim Wesson

SCHOLASTIC

Scholastic Children's Books,
Euston House,
24 Eversholt Street,
London NW1 1DB, UK

A division of Scholastic Ltd
London ~ New York ~ Toronto ~ Sydney ~ Auckland
Mexico City ~ New Delhi ~ Hong Kong

Editorial Director: Lisa Edwards
Editor: Catriona Clarke

Published in the UK by Scholastic Ltd, 2010

Text and illustrations by Nikalas Catlow and Tim Wesson
Text and illustrations © Nikalas Catlow and dogonarock (uk) Ltd, 2010

ISBN 978 1407 11073 8

Printed and bound by Tien Wah Press Pte. Ltd, Singapore

WARNING!

This pirate book is seriously silly!

Pirate luggage mix-up

Captain Crab is ready to set sail. Before he goes, help him match his luggage with its contents.

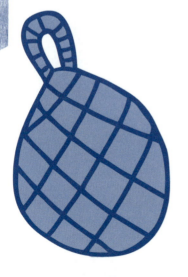

Make your own treasure map

Draw a dotted line for the journey from the ship to the treasure. Add some obstacles and booby traps along the way.

Pirate face shapes

Everything's shipshape matey, ARRR!

Turn everyday stuff into pirate faces!

Pirate pants puzzle

$$💀 + 💀 = 4$$
$$💀 + 💀 = 6$$
$$💀 + 💀 = 10$$
$$💀 + ☠ = 14$$

💀 =

💀 =

💀 =

☠ =

Booty!

Spot five differences.

Draw Bad Bob Big-Pants

We've started you off with his outline.

Feed the sea monster

Kitten Soup

You draw the scenes!

The big cooking pot is bubbling away.

One-eyed Pete tips in a big sack of kittens!

Pete stirs the soup and the kittens bob about.

The kittens look helpless and start mewing.

Show all
the action!

Pete feels sad and
decides to fish them out.

He adds more vegetables
instead.

Pete serves up vegetable soup to the pirates, who
all agree not to eat kitten soup anymore. Hooray!

The crew of the Barmy Barnacle
Colour the shipmates!

A

B

C

D

E

F

G

H

I

Match the crew to their shadows!

Loads of loot

Give each pirate something to carry!

Bad Brian

Brian is sitting on the loo picking his nose.

He's thinking about all the bad stuff he's done...

tee hee

like...

tripping people up,

hiding mice in the fridge,

and scaring the kitten.

Brian laughs so much...

ha ha!

ha ha!

he gets his finger stuck!

I can't go out like this.

Brian tries wiggling his finger...

which tickles his brain...

and makes him think some more...

He thinks things like...

tripping people up can cause an injury,

mice hate living in the fridge,

my kitten is terrified of me.

Brian realizes doing bad stuff is wrong.

Suddenly, his finger pops out!

From now on I will do good stuff instead!

THE END

Pirate pants puzzle

The code is: a=1, b=2, c=3 and so on, through to z=26. Use the code to read the messages on these pages.

1 8 15 25
_ _ _ _

20 8 5 18 5
_ _ _ _ _

8 15 15 11
_ _ _ _

Dot-to-dotty pirate

Join the dots in order!

Buried treasure

Fill the hole with booty!

Show yourself here. ➤

...OR be pulled apart and eaten by a giant crab?

Lucky line maze

Can you hook some treasure, or will you hook a fish instead?

Parrot Poo-Search

What has the greedy parrot been eating? Use the pictures as clues to find the hidden words.

Phew, that's better!

GOLD

g	o	l	d	w	o	y	l
o	w	a	t	c	h	l	c
b	x	y	c	e	a	t	r
l	t	s	w	b	e	e	o
e	b	i	t	y	c	l	w
t	c	o	i	n	s	l	n
e	o	h	u	m	a	y	i
f	p	i	r	a	t	e	g

Create your own pirate parrot.

Find 8 hidden words using the picture clues.

h	u	l	e	v	e	r	n
a	b	a	t	t	e	r	y
m	e	l	b	n	e	q	p
m	t	s	n	s	g	t	s
e	b	a	u	y	c	l	e
r	p	o	i	l	c	a	n
s	m	o	u	s	e	p	g
n	u	t	c	c	h	i	p

CHIP

Piratoku

			1
		2	
	4		
	3		

Fill in the squares so that every row, column and 2 x 2 box contains the numbers 1, 2, 3 and 4. Arrrr, my head hurts!

Create your own hooks!

Greedy Bob
YOU write the story.

Pirate chatter

What are the shipmates saying?

Dot-to-dotty!

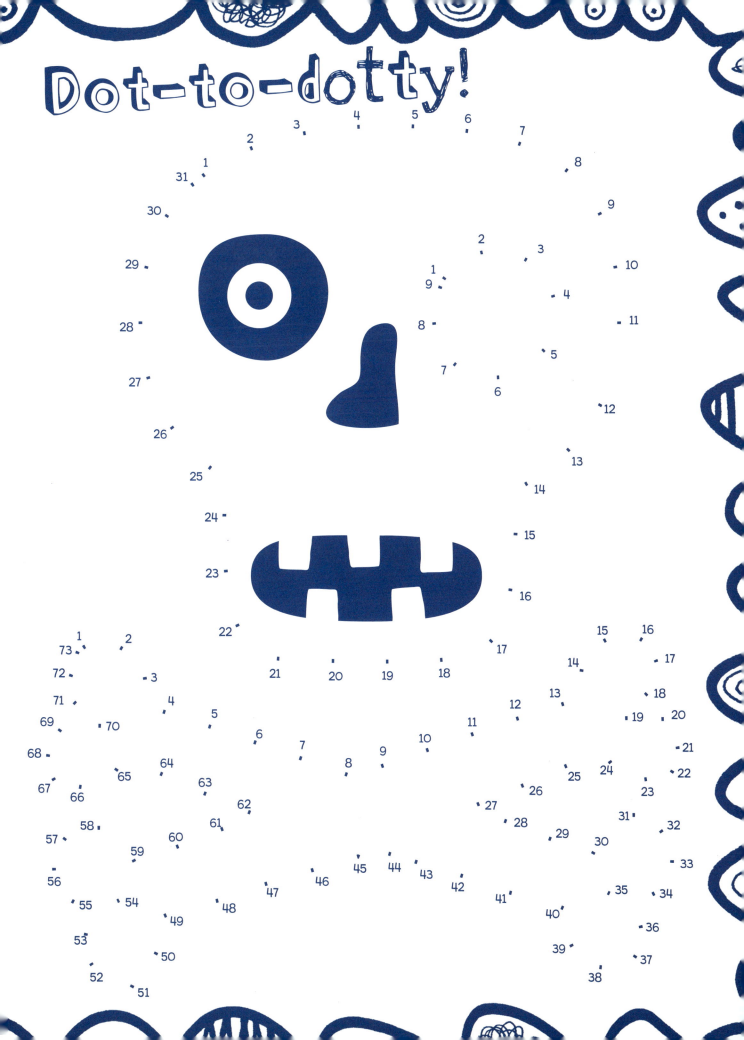

Create your own...

pirate flags

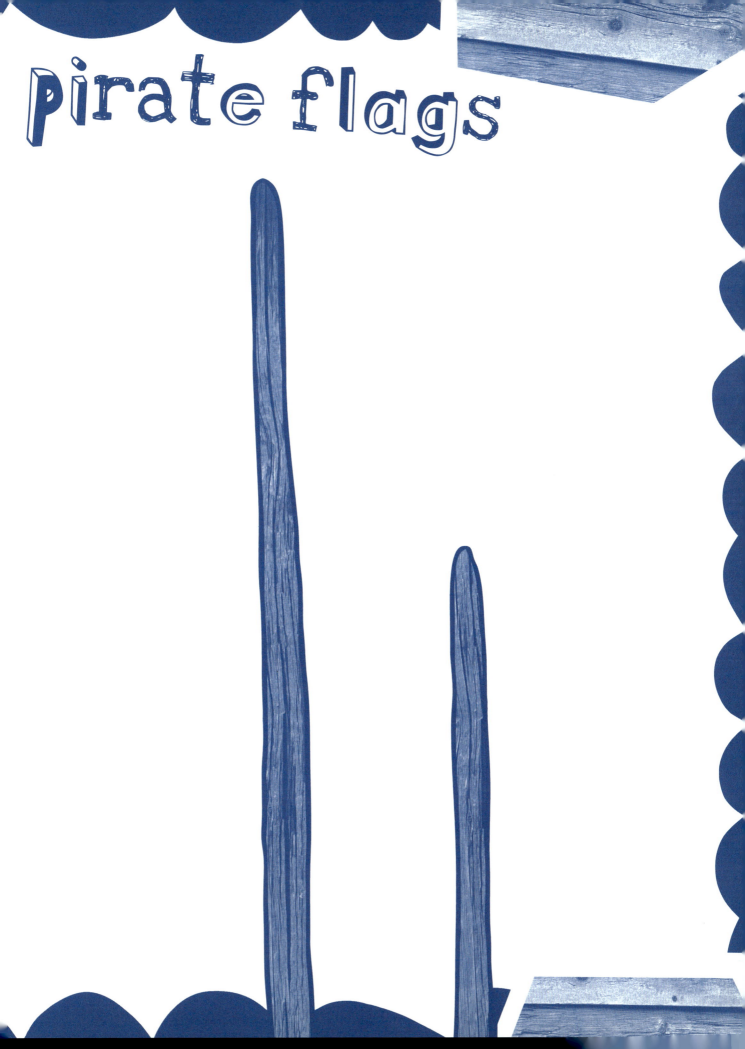

Pete Peg

V

Pirate power: hammering ———— 80

Fighting skill:_ _ _ _ _ _ _ ◯

Strength:_ _ _ _ _ _ _ _ _ ◯

Favourite punishment: _ _ _ _ _ _ _

_ _ _ _ _ _ _ _ _ _ _ _ _ _ _ _ _ _

Parrot-Brain Joe

Pirate power: bird-brainy ———— 80

Fighting skill:_ _ _ _ _ _ _ ◯

Strength:_ _ _ _ _ _ _ _ _ _ ◯

Favourite punishment:_ _ _ _ _ _ _

_ _ _ _ _ _ _ _ _ _ _ _ _ _ _ _

Would you rather

walk the plank with your hands tied...

Draw yourself here.

...OR have your **head pickled?**

Draw your head here.

Specimen:

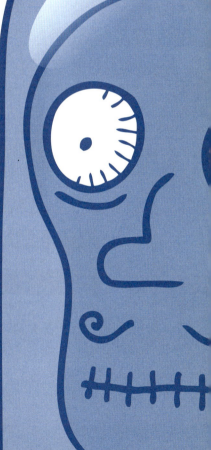

Specimen: pirate

How to be a pirate

1. Dressing like a pirate

...a simple guide to becoming a buccaneer

A trusty pirate wears clothes that are old and ragged.

BEFORE

bandanna

eye patch

baggy shirt (two sizes too big)

belt

crutch (old broom

old boot

peg leg

AFTER

2. A parrot

Pieces of eight! Pieces of eight!

Polly wants a cracker!

Who's a pretty boy?

Get a talking parrot. If you can't find one then use a toy parrot and talk out of the side of your mouth for it.

6. A ship/boat

This can be any kind of ship or boat. You must fly the Jolly Roger.

Cannons are optional but highly recommended.

There she blows!

7. The special pirate walk

BEFORE

AFTER

Finish the crew

Give them silly heads and stupid bodies!

How to draw a pirate

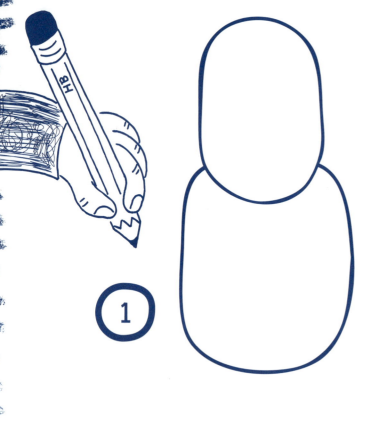

1

2

You can draw the arms and legs in any position you like!

3

4

Create your own pirate here. Aaarrrrr!

The fight!

How many pirates can you see?

Colour them in!

Scurvy dog sea legs

Bad Bob Big-Pants

V

Pirate power: forking —————— 50

Fighting skill: _ _ _ _ _ _

Intelligence: _ _ _ _ _ _ _ _

Favourite punishment: _ _ _ _ _ _ _ _

_ _

Fat Fred Furry-Face

S

Pirate power: dusting ———— 50

Fighting skill: _ _ _ _ _ _ ◯

Intelligence: _ _ _ _ _ _ _ ◯

Favourite punishment: _ _ _ _ _ _ _

_ _ _ _ _ _ _ _ _ _ _ _ _ _ _ _ _

Would you rather

be made to walk the plank into shark-infested custard...

Add some sharks to the custard.

Rigged!

Make use of all the rigging.

Treasure maze

START

Find the buried treasure chest, and pick up booty on the way!

FINISH

Pirate wordsearch

```
c h e s t i x t n
u m a p w m p e u
t g f q z d f l s
l s r l l k t e h
a b x o a c l s i
s f x l g g p c p
s w h o o k g o s
e k b o o t y p i
y j n x r s x e d
```

Draw a pirate

Draw your own pirate character here, using the words from the opposite page.

Piratoku

	3		
		1	
			2
4			

Fill in the squares so that every row, column and 2 x 2 box contains the numbers 1, 2, 3 and 4.

Draw Banana- Barnacle BILL

We've started you off with his outline.

Ahoy shipmate!

Spot the 5 differences!

And now it's time for a...

Seriously silly pirate story

Captain Crab and the crew of the Barmy Barnacle were a bunch of perilous pirates with the silliest names. They were: Fat Fred Furry-Face, Bad Bob Big-Pants, Banana-Barnacle Bill and _____.

Their latest adventure started with a map which Captain Crab had won in a game of _____ at a tavern. 'X marks the spot where the treasure be,' said the Captain, pointing to the map. 'Let's get moving, as I want to be home in time for **The Golden Key**.' That was the Captain's favourite TV show...

Fill in the blanks with silly stuff!

'Fire the cannons!' shouted the Captain. KABOOM! They didn't have any cannonballs so they fired _____ instead.

The pirates arrived at the treasure island, and set off in search of the treasure. They went through the custard swamp, turned left at the whistling rock and right at the _____.

'This is it!' cried Captain Crab. The men started to dig, then suddenly Banana-Barnacle Bill's shovel hit something. Excitedly, he started to dig faster around the object until he revealed a _____. Disappointed, he threw it aside and they carried on digging. Not long after, Bad Bob Big-Pants' shovel hit something too. 'This must be it!' he cried, but it was only a _____.

After more digging they finally found a chest. They pulled it out of the ground and opened it. Inside was a plasma screen TV. 'HURRAH!!' cried Captain Crab. 'Now I can watch The Golden Key in widescreen!'

The End

Horse-Face Harry

Pirate power: pie-throwing ———— 75

Fighting skill:_ _ _ _ _ _ ◯

Strength:_ _ _ _ _ _ _ _ _ _ ◯

Favourite punishment:_ _ _ _ _ _ _ _

_ _

All-Mouth Dave

S

Pirate power: pie-eating ———— 75

Fighting skill:_ _ _ _ _ _

Strength:_ _ _ _ _ _ _ _ _ _

Favourite punishment:_ _ _ _ _ _ _

_ _ _ _ _ _ _ _ _ _ _ _ _ _ _

Beardy weirdy

He's hiding stuff in his beard.

Draw your own pirate
in 4 easy steps...

1.

2.

3.

I like a bit of ARRRRRRRRRT!

Once you've drawn your pirate, why not colour him in?

4.

Draw yours here.

The boat